T h e b e
Recipes from Normandy

Recipes **Brigitte Leroux**

Photographs **Claude Herlédan**

Translated by **Atlantique Traduction**

Recipes made by apprentices of the catering
section at the I.C.E.P. Caen.

Editions OUEST-FRANCE

No one is ever disappointed by Normandy cuisine. A magnificent and secret land, Normandy offers authentic produce from its breezy coastline to its hinterland of rolling hills, wooded farmland and orchard meadows through which trout streams wind mellifluously. A region famed for its dairy produce, whose cookery would not be the same without its cream, so beautiful and so full of flavour, and its butter with its fruity taste. And its cheeses! Whose mouth has not watered at the sight of a Camembert, a Pont l'Evêque or a Livarot... and there are many more. Game of the highest quality, meat from the salt-marshes, seafood always freshly available, deliciously drinkable cider, and a brandy, Calvados, which is out of this world: here lies its magic. Don't fool around with its soul, Normandy cuisine will not forgive you.
A generous cuisine, a cuisine of quality and of inventiveness.
Don't skimp on the produce and you will be well rewarded. This is a small book and choices had to be made which was a very difficult job!

Mère **Poulard's** *omelette*

Ingredients for 4 people:

8 eggs (new laid),
2 tablespoons crème fraîche,
30 g butter,
salt, pepper,
herbs (parsley, chervil, tarragon)

There are several variations of the omelette known as "Mont-Saint-Michel". It can be filled with mushrooms, green or smoked bacon, shrimps or mussels, for example. Here is a simple and tasty recipe: Mère Poulard's omelette. But do not forget that to make a successful omelette, you should always use a good frying pan, with a heavy base and kept spotlessly clean.

Separate the yolks from the whites.

Take two soup plates. In one beat the yolks with freshly ground salt and pepper.

In the other, whisk the whites as for an ordinary omelette. It is not necessary to whisk them stiffly.

In a flat-bottomed frying pan, melt a good-sized knob of butter and when it begins to sizzle, pour in the yolks.

Lightly whip the cream in a bowl and wait until the yolks are nearly set before covering them with it.

Add the whites straight away.

The omelette should be cooked on a high heat and should take no more than three minutes.

Fold the omelette over and slide it on to a warmed, long serving dish.

Sprinkle with melted butter and finely chopped herbs.

Mère Poulard's omelette.

Vegetable Soup with Bacon.

Vegetable Soup *with Bacon*

Ingredients for 6 people:

3 potatoes,
3 carrots,
3 turnips,
3 leeks,
3 small onions,
1 clove of garlic,
150 g lean bacon,
100 g crème fraîche,
30 g butter,
2 litres chicken stock,
salt, pepper,
croûtons of stale bread

Wash and peel all the vegetables. Chop them finely, except for the onions, which should be sliced into thin rounds.
Melt the butter in a large saucepan and sweat all the chopped vegetables in it for about five minutes.
Finely dice the bacon. Add it to the vegetables. Cook gently for about ten minutes.
Heat the chicken stock and when it is very hot, pour it over the vegetables.
Cook over a low heat for about an hour, and, because of the bacon, season only lightly with salt, but with plenty of pepper.
Rub the warmed tureen with the garlic.
Put a few croûtons of stale bread in the bottom. Cover with the crème fraîche and pour in the boiling soup. Do not stir!
Sprinkle with freshly chopped parsley.It's jolly good...

Cream of Mussel Soup

In Normandy, we call large mussels "culs-bleus" (blue-bottoms), but for this dish we prefer to use the mussels from Isigny or Lion-sur-Mer, which are smaller and whiter and have a more delicate flavour.

Ingredients for 6 people:

2 litres mussels,
100 g cultivated mushrooms,
2 leeks,
1 glass white wine,
1 shallot,
1 onion,
2 rounded tablespoons flour,
40 g butter,
2 egg yolks,
2 tablespoons crème fraîche, parsley,
salt, pepper

Carefully wash the leeks. Keep the white part only. Chop them as finely as possible.

Prepare the mushrooms: wash quickly in water and trim and discard the base of the stems. Mince very finely.

Scrape and wash the mussels in plenty of water. Put them into a large saucepan with a glass of white wine, the onion and the peeled shallot, and a few sprigs of parsley and cook on a high heat for a few minutes until the mussels are open.

Remove the mussels from their shell, taking care to save their cooking liquor.

Strain this liquor through a very fine sieve. In a large, heavy-bottomed saucepan, combine the flour and the butter using a wooden spatula.

Pour in the cooking liquor from the mussels (the onion, shallot and parsley will already have been discarded), and a litre of water.

To this stock add the minced mushrooms and leeks. Season very lightly with salt, but generously with pepper.

Bring to the boil.

Cook for 30 minutes. Then add the mussels, which should only be cooked for a very short time to keep them tender.

Scald the tureen.

Combine the crème fraîche with the two egg yolks.

Pour this mixture into the serving dish and add the soup a little at a time, stirring constantly.

Serve this delicious cream soup very hot.

Sweet omelette with calvados

Ingredients for 4 people:

8 large eggs,
150 g of sugar,
30 g of butter,
8 cl of calvados,
salt

Break the eggs into a bowl. Add the sugar and a pinch of salt.

Beat briskly.

Melt the butter in a pan and add the beaten eggs. Toss the pan continuously while moulding the mixture.

When cooked, roll the omelette onto a pretty serving dish.

Heat the calvados in a small pan, light and pour over the dessert immediately before serving.

Cream of Mussel Soup.

Farmer's wife terrine *with calvados*

Ingredients for 8 people:

400 g of chicken livers,
450 g of farm pork spare ribs,
200 g of streaky bacon fat,
17.5 cl of single cream,
10 cl of calvados,
salt (about 25 g) and milled black pepper.

Carefully remove the nerves from the chicken livers. Pour over the calvados and leave to marinate for two hours in a cool place.

Mince all the meat, medium grid.

Gently fold this mincemeat with the cream and the marinade juice. Season with salt and pepper to taste.

Fill the terrine with the mix. Use a spatula to form an even surface.

Cover and place in a bain-marie. Cook for one hour in a hot oven (gas mark 6/7) with the lid on, followed by fifteen minutes with the lid removed. Check the grease around the pâté, when it is clear, the terrine is ready.

Leave this excellent terrine for at least two or three days before eating.

Camembert Croquettes.

Camembert Croquettes

Ingredients for 4 people:

1 camembert, not too ripe, 2 eggs, 2 tablespoons crème fraîche, flour, breadcrumbs, cayenne pepper, nutmeg

To prepare the Sauce Normande:

In a heavy-bottomed pan, fry a finely chopped onion in 30 g butter until it is golden. Add 30 g of flour and the same amount of butter.

Work together with a wooden spatula. When the roux is well-thickened, add a quarter of a litre of dry cider. Beat the mixture thoroughly and season with salt, pepper and a pinch of nutmeg. Away from the heat, incorporate a quarter of a litre of crème fraîche and a dash of lemon juice.

To make the Croquettes:

Crush the Camembert with a fork. Mix in 3 tablespoons of the Sauce Normande to soften it and mix it with some of the crème fraîche.

Beat the eggs in a bowl.

Shape the croquettes, dip them in the beaten egg, then roll in the flour and lastly, the breadcrumbs.

Fry in hot oil until they are a beautiful golden brown.

Drain on kitchen paper and serve with a Normandy-style lettuce salad.

Marrow fondue with cream

Ingredients for 6 people:

*1 nice marrow about **3.5 kg** (not too ripe), **200 g** of freshly grated Gruyère cheese, **8** square slices of bread, **1** litre of whipping cream, salt and milled pepper.*

Preheat oven (high temperature, gas mark 7/8).

Toast the slices of bread.

Cut each in quarters to make croutons.

Cut out a large section of the top of the marrow and very carefully remove the seeds from the inside.

Place several croutons into the bottom of the marrow.

Layer with the grated Gruyère and croutons alternately.

Lightly season the cream with salt and pepper and pour into the marrow. Close marrow with its top.

Place on a dripping pan and into the oven. Bake for two hours.

Serve piping hot. It looks and tastes good!

Black Pudding on a bed of apples.

Black Pudding *on a* bed *of apples*

Ingredients for 4 people:

1 large piece black pudding,
5 good apples, firm fleshed and slightly sharp (Reinettes, for example),
30 g butter,
1 liqueur glass Calvados,
1 tablespoon oil,
a pinch of cinnamon,
salt,
pepper

Black pudding, which is particularly rich in iron, is made with coagulated pig's blood to which is added pork fat, onions and various spices, from which it derives its variety of flavour.

Peel and core the apples. Cut into even slices about 5 mm thick. Melt the butter in a frying pan and when it is hot, put in the apples.

Turn the slices of fruit from time to time using a wooden spatula. When they are a really golden brown, season them with a touch of cinnamon, salt and pepper.

Keep them warm.

Brush the black pudding with a little oil and prick the skin. Grill it on all sides at medium heat.

Drain it on kitchen paper.

In a flameproof earthenware casserole, arrange the black pudding in a coil, enthroned on the apples. Return to the heat.

Just before serving, pour the Calvados over and set alight.

Camembert tagliatelli

Ingredients for 4 people:

400 g of tagliatelli (or spaghetti)
1 "fully ripe" camembert,
100 g of halved walnuts,
20 cl of single cream,
salt and milled pepper.

Boil the pasta in a large pan of salted water.

Meanwhile, remove the camembert rind. Cut into small pieces before slowly melting with the cream in a heavy-based saucepan.

Roughly crush the walnuts.

Drain the tagliatelli before placing into a preheated shallow serving dish.

Pour the camembert cream over the pasta. Add the crushed walnuts. Season with a few turns of the pepper mill.

Usually, there is no need for salt as the camembert is salty enough.

Mix carrefully before serving immediatly.

Bayeux-style Chitterlings

Ingredients for 4 people:

4 chitterlings,
4 dsp fresh cream,
2 tablespoons strong mustard,
2 sprigs fresh tarragon,
salt.

Light grill and set to medium heat.

Score chitterlings so that skins do not burst during cooking.

Wrap separately in aluminium foil and grill for approximately 20 minutes, turning once during cooking.

While chitterlings are cooking, wash tarragon, remove leaves from stem and chop finely.

Blend fresh cream and mustard with a wooden spoon in a thick-bottomed saucepan and heat gently over low heat. Taste and add salt if required. Do not add pepper. Stir in chopped tarragon.

Remove chitterlings from grill. Remove from foil and lay out on serving dish.

Serve sauce separately in a scalded sauceboat.

This is a delicious meal and can be served with a plain, unsweetened apple puree.

Normandy-style Lettuce *salad*

In a salad bowl, make the vinaigrette dressing with a little cider vinegar and some thick crème fraîche.

Season with a pinch of salt and pepper. Taste and adjust seasoning if necessary.

Carefully wash and dry a good lettuce grown in open ground.

Add the lettuce to the dressing. So as not to wilt it, do not toss until ready to serve.

Fillets *of* sole *with* apples

Ingredients for 4 people:

4 good sole fillets,
7 really sharp apples,
3 shallots,
150 g butter,
25 cl crème fraîche,
2 glasses dry cider,
25 cl fish stock (prepared in advance),
salt and pepper.

Wipe the fillets with a cloth soaked in salt water.

Peel all the apples. Keep four of them for the garnish.

Core the others and cut into large dice.

In a heavy bottomed pan, heat a good-sized knob of butter until it turns golden. Add the diced apples and cover with a glass of cider.

After a few minutes of gentle cooking, mash into a purée.

Finely chop the shallots.

Melt a little butter in a large frying pan and put in the chopped shallots. Cook gently for two minutes, but without letting them colour.

Place the sole fillets on the bed of cooked shallots. Season with salt and pepper. Pour over the second glass of cider and the fish stock. Cover and continue to cook gently for about a quarter of an hour.

Meanwhile, core the other apples. Cut them into quarters. Heat the rest of the butter in a casserole and brown the quartered fruit, stirring gently. When they are cooked, put them aside and keep warm.

Bring the apple/cider purée to the boil. Add the crème fraîche. Mix well. Then cook over a low heat, stirring constantly.

Pour into a sauceboat. Keep warm.

Warm the serving dish and arrange the drained sole fillets on it.

Reduce the cooking liquor on high heat and strain it. Sprinkle these delicious juices over the fish. Arrange the apple quarters around it and serve immediately, with the sauce separately.

As a drink to accompany this dish, serve the farmhouse cider used in its preparation.

Plaice in cider

Fillets of sole with apples.

Plaice *in* **cider**

Ingredients for 4 people:

1 good plaice weighing 800 g,
4 shallots,
1 glass breadcrumbs,
2 glasses cider,
herbs (parsley, chervil, tarragon, chives),
1 knob of butter,
1 ladle of cream,
salt, pepper

Wash the fish, which should be prepared by the fishmonger, in salt water. Wipe it dry.
Chop the shallots and the herbs.
Butter a large baking dish and spead the shallots and the herbs over the bottom.
Lay the fish on top and cover with cider.
Season with salt and pepper and sprinkle with breadcrumbs.
Put in a medium oven and cook for about fifteen minutes.
A little before the end of the cooking time, add the cream and just before serving, sprinkle with herbs again.

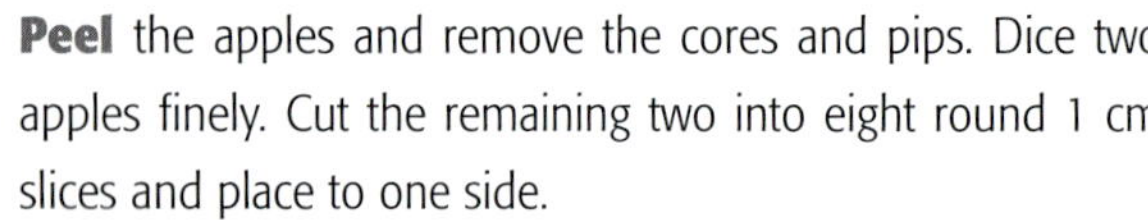

Monkfish **tournedos** *with pommeau and calvados*

Ingredients for 4 people:

4 nice **200 g** *monkfish steaks (prepared by the fishmonger),*
4 *rennet apples,*
1 *shallot,*
80 g *of butter,*
30 cl *of double cream,*
6 cl *of calvados,*
6 cl *of pommeau,*
salt, milled pepper.

Peel the apples and remove the cores and pips. Dice two apples finely. Cut the remaining two into eight round 1 cm slices and place to one side.

Peel the shallot and chop finely.

Melt a large part of the butter in a large heavy-based saucepan. Sweat the chopped shallot with the diced apples.

Heat the calvados, flambé and add to the shallot and diced apples. Mix well before flavouring with the pommeau.

Add the cream and mix. Reduce the sauce on a low heat for 5 min.

Mix the sauce in a mixer before passing it through a conical strainer. Taste before seasoning with salt and milled pepper. Keep warm.

Heat a little olive oil in a casserole dish. Season the monkfish slices with salt and pepper before cooking for fifteen minutes, turning carefully when half done.

Meanwhile, heat a large knob of butter and brown the apple slices.

Dress each preheated plate with a slice of monkfish, flanked by two apple slices.

Coat nicely with the sauce and serve with rice, fresh spinach and steamed small courgettes.

Poached **Cherbourg** *Lobster*

Ingredients for 4 people:

4 *small lobsters (approx.* **300 g** *each),*
150 g *butter,*
1 *dsp. fresh cream,*
juice of **1** *lemon,*
3 *carrots,*
few drops wine vinegar,
1 *small glass dry white wine,*
1 *bouquet garni (thyme, bay, parsley),*
salt,
pepper.

Peel carrots and cut into slices. Place carrots and bouquet garni in large pan.

Pour in two litres cold water, add few drops vinegar and small glass dry white wine.

Add handful sea salt and a few pepper corms.

When carrots are cooked, place lobster in boiling court bouillon and cook over high heat for approximately 15 minutes.

Meanwhile, pour lemon juice into small saucepan, add fresh cream and bring to boil.

Gradually blend in butter cut into pieces.

Season with salt and pepper and boil for two minutes, stirring all the time.

Scald sauceboat with hot water and pour sauce into it.

Remove bouquet garni from court bouillon.

Lay each lobster in soup plate.

Pour on some of warm court bouillon and serve with hot butter sauce.

Brill in a **shrimp** *and mussel sauce from* **Dieppe**

Ingredients for 4 people:

1 brill, about 1 kg, prepared by the fishmonger,
150 g peeled shrimps,
1 litre mussels,
100 g cultivated mushrooms
150 g crème fraîche,
100 g butter,
2 lemons,
3 dl dry white wine,
salt, pepper,
herbs (parsley, chervil, chives).

Brill in a shrimp and mussel sauce, from Dieppe

Remove the black skin from the brill, if the fishmonger has not done it. Run a sharp knife down the lateral line to the bone.

Generously butter the inside of a shallow baking dish. Sprinkle with freshly chopped herbs.

Season the brill on both sides with salt and pepper and place in the baking dish.

Pour over the white wine and dot the fish with butter before baking in a hot oven.

Cook for about twenty minutes.

Meanwhile, scrape and wash the mussels in plenty of water. Put them in a large pan and cook over a high heat to open them. When they have opened take them off the heat and remove the shells.

Clean the mushrooms (wash them quickly and cut off the rough part of the stem). Slice them. In a saucepan, melt a large knob of butter. Add the mushrooms and sprinkle with the juice of one lemon.

Cook on a low heat for 10 minutes. When the fish is cooked, keep it warm on its serving dish.

Strain the mushrooms' cooking liquor and thin with the cream. Then add the juice of the other lemon.

Pour this sauce into the dish in which the fish was cooked and stir well. Taste and adjust seasoning if necessary.

Arrange the mussels, the peeled shrimps and the mushrooms around the fish and cover with this magnificent sauce.

Fish fillets *poached in a* **white wine** *from the* **Caux area**

Ingredients for 4 people:

10 fish fillets
(monkfish, sole, dab, whiting)
25 cl dry white wine,
2 carrots,
2 leeks,
1 onion,
1 bouquet garni (parsley, thyme, bayleaf),
salt, peppercorns.

For the sauce:
10 g flour,
75 g butter,
50 cl dry cider,
1/2 lemon,
1 onion,
1 heaped tablespoon cream, salt, pepper
pinch of nutmeg.

Into a large saucepan, put a quarter of a litre of water and the same quantity of white wine. Put in all the fish fillets.
Chop the carrots and leeks. Put them and the bouquet garni into the saucepan. Season with salt and a few peppercorns. Bring to the boil.
Cover and simmer for half an hour.
Remove from the heat and allow to cool uncovered so that the liquid reduces.
Arrange the pieces of fish on a deep, oval dish. Pass the cooking liquor through a very fine sieve. If it is not strong enough, reduce again, uncovered on a high heat. Pour this stock over the fillets and keep warm.
Peel and chop the onion. Fry it gently in a little melted butter on a low heat.
Add the rest of the butter and the flour. Stir well with a wooden spatula. The onion should not colour during cooking. Pour in the cider.
Season with salt pepper and a pinch of nutmeg.
Continue cooking for another ten minutes on a low heat.
Then thin with the cream and flavour with a few drops of lemon juice.
Cover the fish with this marvellous sauce, typical of the Caux area, and serve immediately.

Caux-style **Skate**

Ingredients for 4 people:

4 good-sized pieces crimped skate,
125 g butter,
125 g fresh cream,
2 egg yolks,
few drops vinegar,
1 large bunch parsley,
salt,
pepper.

Wash pieces of skate under running water and steam till cooked. Remove skin and crimped edge of skate.
Lay pieces of skate on warm serving dish. Add few drops of vinegar to each piece.
In a thick-bottomed saucepan, melt butter and cream over low heat, stirring continuously with a wooden spoon.
Season with salt and pepper.
Carefully wash bunch of parsley and chop finely.
Remove saucepan from heat, bind sauce with two egg yolks and add freshly-chopped parsley.
Pour the creamy sauce over fish and serve immediately.

Fish fillets poached in white wine, from the Caux area

Scallops in white sauce

Ingredients for 6 people:

20 scallops in their shells with roe (choose firmly closed, clean scallops),
250 g cultivated mushrooms,
50 g butter,
2 dl crème fraîche,
1 egg,
2 onions,
1 tablespoon flour,
1 clove garlic,
1/4 litre dry white wine,
1 liqueur glass Calvados,
salt, pepper,
4 spice powder (cinnamon, clove, nutmeg, pepper).

Scallops in white sauce

To prepare the scallops: put the scallop on a cloth folded in four, with the flat side uppermost. Cut the muscle inside by slipping a strong-bladed knife between the two shells.

Cut the beards (the gristly grey part which surrounds the white part) and remove the black pouch. Keep only the white part and the roe. Wipe with a damp cloth. (The beards can be used in the preparation of fish stock).

Clean the mushrooms carefully but quickly, as they should not get wet. Remove the rough end of the stem and slice evenly.

Peel the garlic and the onions. Crush the garlic with a fork and chop the onions very finely. In a high-sided frying pan, melt the butter and over a high heat, throw in the scallops. Their flesh should become firm but not coloured.

Pour the Calvados over and set alight! Add the minced onion, cover and cook very gently until soft.

Then dust with flour. Stir well. Cover with the white wine and an equal amount of water. (Ideally, the water should be replaced with fish stock. There are some excellent ones produced commercially).

Add the crushed garlic and the spices. Cook for fifteen minutes.

Meanwhile, fry the sliced mushrooms in a very little butter and add to the scallops.

In a bowl, mix together the crème fraîche and the yolk of an egg.

Pour it over the scallop mixture. Stir and continue cooking for three minutes. The sauce must not boil.

Warm some small dishes. Pour in the cooked scallops and serve.

Large scallop *purses*

Ingredients for 4 people:

4 feuilles de brick (hard wheat pancakes),
3 golden delicious apples,
12 white flesh of scallops,
30 g of butter,
1 green leek leaf,
olive oil,
salt and pepper.

Blanch the leek leaf for one minute before cooling under a trickle of water.

Cut into four straight thin strips.

Peel the apples. Remove the cores and pips before dicing into small cubes.

Brown the diced apple in very hot butter and place in hot place.

Carefully dry the scallop flesh before quickly frying in the olive oil to give them a nice colour.

Lightly season with salt and pepper.

Roll the "feuilles de brick" on the work surface.

Place the diced apples onto the centre of each "feuille", followed by the scallop flesh.

Close each "feuille de brick" to form the shape of a purse and tie with the leek laces.

Brush the four purses with melted butter.

Bake in hot oven (gas mark 6/7) for 10 minutes. Check baking constantly.

Serve these tempting crusty purses hot.

Country cod

Ingredients for 4 people:

4 200 g cod steaks,
1 litre of mussels,
150 g of cooked prawns,
3 small shallots,
200 button mushrooms,
10 cl of dry cider,
250 g of double cream,
50 g of butter,
1 bunch of parsley, salt and pepper.

Preheat oven to gas mark 6.

Remove the sandy part of the mushrooms. Wash quickly before slicing finely.

Peel and chop the shallots finely.

Butter a large deep ovenproof dish. Cover the bottom with the chopped shallots, sliced mushrooms and cubes of butter and place the cod steaks on top.

Cover with large knobs of cream. Add the cider. Season with salt and a few turns of the pepper mill.

Bake for thirty minutes, basting several times during cooking. Meanwhile, peel the prawns, retaining only the tails.

Scrape the mussels under running water. Place in a stockpot with a litter water and over a high heat, warm them while shaking briskly for 4 to 5 min until they open.

Remove from pot and strain the juice through muslin.

When the fish is cooked, place the prawn tails and mussels onto the cooking dish. Deglaze with the mussel juice.

Sprinkle this excellent fish dish with chopped parsley before serving immediatly with a few steamed potatoes.

Bessin-style Trout

Gut and carefully wipe fish.

Pour milk into soup plate. Add copious quantity of salt and quickly dip fish into milk then roll in flour.

Heat large knob of butter in large frying pan. Fry trout over medium heat. Cooking trout requires some care and they should not be cooked for more than 7 to 8 minutes on each side.

Make sure that you do not prick the fish as you turn them over.

When fish are cooked, pour on Calvados and set alight. Add cream. Leave to boil for a minute or two then pour in lemon juice. Season with salt and give added flavour with pinch of freshly-ground nutmeg.

Ingredients for 4 people:

4 good-sized trouts,
flour,
milk,
butter,
juice of 1 lemon,
5 cl Calvados (apple brandy),
salt, pepper,
nutmeg.

Normandy stuffed turkey

Ingredients for 6 to 8 people:

1 turkey,
*about **3 kg** (plucked and dressed),*
2 tablespoons oil.

For the stuffing:
***300 g** chicken livers,*
***300 g** sausagemeat,*
***300 g** onions,*
1 liqueur glass Calvados,
salt, pepper.

For the stock:
any vegetable is allowed! (mushrooms, carrots, leeks, potatoes, turnips, celery, radishes, cauliflower, French beans, tomatoes, etc.),
2 litres of very dry cider,
1 glass Calvados,
salt, pepper.

For the garnish:
6 to 8 Reinette apples,
***150 g** butter.*

Normandy stuffed turkey

Peel and finely chop the onions. Mince the chicken livers. Dice the peeled and cored apples.
Melt a large knob of butter in a frying pan. Fry the sausagemeat, the chopped onions and chicken livers and the diced apples quickly.
Cover with the Calvados. Season the stuffing with salt and pepper. Fill the body cavity of the bird with this mixture and sew up the opening.
Brush the turkey with oil. Season with salt and pepper. Brown it all over on a high heat.
Into a large saucepan, pour the cider and Calvados. Add the vegetables, peeled and cut into chunks, salt and pepper.
Put the bird into this stock and cook for about an hour and a half. The cooking time depends on the size of the turkey. Using the point of a knife, prick the meat from time to time to check how much it has cooked. Cover.
Shortly before the end of the cooking time, peel and core the apples. Cut into quarters and fry in butter until golden. Set aside in a warm place.
Remove the turkey from the stock and cut into pieces. Warm the serving dish.
Pour all the cream into the saucepan and boil for half an hour. It must be left uncovered to reduce the liquid.
Stir to obtain a nice smooth purée.
Arrange the turkey pieces on the serving dish, garnished with the apple quarters seasoned with salt and pepper.
Cover plentifully with this wonderful sauce.

Young **pigeons** *in cider*

Cider, an alcoholic drink, of a golden or reddish colour, is generally made from 1/3 sweet apples and 2/3 sharp apples, and it can be sweet and sugary or dry or bitter. It can be still, fizzy or sparkling. It can be drunk from the beginning to the end of a meal, but it does not go at all well with game. Although a good, very dry cider... For this recipe we would use a rough cider, as is still produced on farms.

Ingredients for 4 people:

4 young pigeons,
1 liqueur glass Calvados,
1 glass very dry cider,
150 g butter,
thyme,
bayleaf,
salt,
pepper.

Ask your game dealer to dress and truss the pigeons. (To truss a pigeon: the use of cooking string to keep its wings and legs in place during cooking).

Sizzle a knob of butter in a casserole and when it is starting to turn golden, put in the pigeons and brown all over (do not hesitate to turn them often), on a high heat.

Season with salt, pepper, a pinch of thyme and a bayleaf.

Pour the Calvados over and set alight!

Cover and continue cooking on low heat, for half an hour.

Keep the birds warm, on a serving dish.

Deglaze the meat juices left stuck to the bottom of the pan with the glass of cider. Use a wooden spatula. There should be none left behind!

Bring to the boil and boil for two minutes.

Away from the heat, add some knobs of butter to smoothen this lovely brown sauce.

Pour over the pigeons and serve accompanied by simple baked apples.

Young pigeons in cider

Chicken with cream and Calvados, from the Auge Valley

Chicken with cream and **calvados** from the **Auge Valley**

Ingredients for 4 people:

*1 free-range chicken, about **1.2 kg**, jointed,*
80 g butter,
150 g crème fraîche,
1 egg yolk,
750 g cultivated mushrooms,
1/2 lemon,
1 liqueur glass Calvados,
salt, pepper.

Brown the chicken joints in a large cast iron casserole, in 30 g of hot, melted butter. Keep the heat high to obtain a fine golden brown colour.

Season with freshly ground salt and pepper.

Add 10 cl water. Cover and simmer for a good half an hour. Meanwhile, prepare the mushrooms. Remove the rough part of the stems and wash the mushrooms quickly. Slice evenly.

Heat the rest of the butter in a frying pan until golden. Fry the mushrooms in it on a high heat.

Sprinkle with the juice of half a lemon to stop them discolouring, and cook for another five minutes.

When the chicken is cooked, pour the Calvados over and set it alight!

Set the pieces to one side and warm the serving dish.

Deglaze the bottom of the casserole with the crème fraîche and thicken with the egg yolk.

Cover the chicken pieces with this delicious, truly golden sauce and arrange the cooked mushrooms round them.

Pays d'Auge **veal** chops

Ingredients for 4 people:

4 cow-reared veal chops,
1 kg of fresh French beans,
250 g of button mushrooms,
100 g of butter,
100 g of double cream,
25 cl of calvados,
10 cl of dry cider,
salt and milled pepper.

Remove the sandy part of the mushrooms before washing quickly in slightly vinegared water. Slice evenly.
String the French beans and wash carefully.
Bring a large pan of salted water to the boil before adding the French beans to cook "al dente", i.e. they remain slightly crunchy. Place to one side.
Season the veal chops generously with salt and pepper before browning them on each side in browned butter.
In another pan, lightly fry the mushrooms in butter. Place to one side. When the meat is cooked, pour the calvados into the pan, light and flambé.
Dress serving plate with the veal chops and place in a warm place. Meanwhile, in the pan used for cooking the mushrooms, reduce the cider by half before adding the cream and mushrooms.
Mix carefully then bring to the boil. Leave on low heat for 2 to 3 minutes.
Slowly reheat the French beans in a little butter. Season with salt and pepper. Dress the veal chops with the French beans before coating generously with the sauce.
It's very tasty!

Veal **kidneys** flamed with **calvados**

Ingredients for 4 people:

4 small veal kidneys, prepared by the butcher,
3 granny smith apples,
1 large onion,
1 glass of calvados,
10 cl double cream,
80 g of butter,
1 tablespoon of strong mustard,
salt and milled pepper.

Dice the kidneys into large cubes. Peel and finely chop the onion. Heat a large knob of butter and gently brown the chopped onion.
Wash and dry the apples. Without peeling, remove the cores and pips. Cut into quarters.
Add the apple quarters to the onion. Lightly salt, cover and continue to cook on a low heat, stirring occasionally. When the apples are cooked, place into a mixer with the onions and mix until puréed. Leave in hot place.
In a deep frying pan, quickly sauté the veal kidney cubes in browned butter (3 to 4 min). Flambé with the calvados. Remove the veal kidney cubes from the cooking juices, season with salt and a few turns of the pepper mill and leave in a hot place. Deglaze the cooking juices with the cream and without heating, add the mustard.
Mix carefully, using a spatula to gently scrape the bottom of the pan before passing the sauce through a conical strainer. Warm the plates. Dress the centre of each with the veal kidneys and surround with the apple and onion purée before coating with the savoury sauce.

Boiled leg of **lamb** *from Yvetot*

Ingredients for 6 people:

__2 kg__ leg of lamb,
__1 kg__ carrots,
__8__ leeks,
__500 g__ turnips,
__3__ onions stuck with cloves,
__1__ good bouquet garni (thyme, bayleaf, parsley, a stick of celery),
__2__ cloves of garlic,
salt,
a dash of Calvados

For the sauce:
__160 g__ butter,
__100 g__ flour,
__50 cl__ stock,
__25 cl__ crème fraîche,
capers

Our English friends serve it with mint sauce.
Could William the Conqueror have left them this old Norman recipe which was enjoyed by the King of Yvetot?

In a large pan of water, simmer the carrots, leeks, turnips, onions and bouquet garni for a good hour. Add salt and flavour with a dash of Calvados.
Rub the lamb with the garlic.
After the hour's simmering, put the lamb into the stock and continue to cook for an hour and a half. In a heavy-bottomed pan, make a roux with the flour and butter.
Thin it down with 50 cl of the stock in which the lamb and vegetables have been cooked.
Cook gently for a few minutes. Then, away from the heat, add the crème fraîche and the capers. Pour into a sauceboat.
Serve this wonderful leg of lamb on a long platter, garnished with its carrots, turnips and leeks.

Boiled leg of lamb, from Yvetot

Normandy braised beef

Ingredients for 4 people:

1 kg piece of chuck beef,
1 calf's foot,
2 pork rinds,
1 kg carrots,
1 onion stuck with cloves,
1 clove garlic,
30 g butter,
1 half-litre dry white wine,
1 bouquet garni (parsley, thyme, bayleaf),
parsley,
salt, pepper.

Make a marinade with the white wine, the onion, the carrots sliced in rounds, the garlic crushed with a fork and the bouquet garni.

Tie the meat and marinade overnight.

Afterwards, drain it and melt a good-sized knob of butter in a cast iron casserole. Put in the beef and fry it all over in the butter. It should be well browned.

Remove the carrots from the marinade. Strain the liquor and pour over the meat. If there is not enough marinade, add a little water. The piece of beef should be completely covered by liquid.

Add the calf's foot, the pork rind and the carrots. Season with salt and pepper.

Cover and as soon as it comes to the boil, remove from the heat and finish the cooking in a medium oven for about two hours.

Serve the joint surrounded by carrots sprinkled with finely chopped parsley.

Normandy braised beef

Normandy fruit salad

Normandy **fruit** *salad*

Ingredients for 4 people:

3 pears,
3 apples,
12 greengages,
split almonds,
100 g sugar,
1 liqueur glass Calvados,
25 cl crème fraîche,
10 g butter

Wash, dry, and halve the greengages. Discard the stones. Peel the apples and pears.

Slice the fruit evenly, taking care to remove cores and seeds.

Clean thc raspberries (without washing).

Put all the fruit into a pretty glass fruit bowl.

Dust with sugar and sprinkle with Calvados. Stir very carefully so as not to damage the fruit.

Macerate in the refrigerator for two hours.

Melt a knob of butter in a saucepan and fry the split almonds. Shake the pan vigorously so that the almonds brown all over.

Cover the fruit salad with crème fraîche, without stirring!

Decorate with grilled almonds and serve very cold.

Glazed apples with calvados

Ingredients for 4 people:

4 rennet apples,
60 g of butter,
caster sugar,
calvados.

Preheat oven to gas mark 6/7.
Peel the apples and remove the cores before placing in a buttered grain dish.
Gently melt the butter. It should not brown at all.
Sprinkle the apples with the melted butter before sprinkling copiously with sugar.
Place the gratin dish into hot oven and bake the fruits for 15 min. When the apples are cooked, dress 4 pretty dishes with an apple each.
Flambé the calvados and pour the fruity alcohol over each apple.
Serve immediately.

Auntie Carol's cake

Ingredients for 4 people:

3 or 4 sour apples,
100 g of sieved flour,
150 g of caster sugar,
50 g of unsalted butter,
2 large eggs,
1 teaspoon of baker's yeast.

Butter a sponge cake tin.
Peel the apples, remove the cores and slice into even strips.
In a bowl, beat the eggs and mix in the sugar before mixing in the sieved flour with the yeast.
Gently melt the butter and add to the mixture when barely tepid. Beat the mixture firmly with a wooden spatula until very smooth. Add the apple slices and mix carefully.
Pour into the cake tin and bake immediately in a medium oven for about 30 min. It is easy and quick to make, and really nice if the ingredients are chosen with care.

Pear dessert flamed with calvados

Ingredients for 6 people:

6 pears,
50 g sliced almonds,
80 g caster sugar,
80 g icing sugar,
2 egg whites,
30 g butter,
5 cl Calvados (apple brandy),
1 pinch salt.

Peel pears, remove cores and pips. Cut into slices and dust with caster sugar.
Heat butter in pan and gently cook fruit for 5 minutes.
Pour on Calvados and set alight, ensuring that brandy runs over all slices of pear. Then lay fruit out in an attractive oven-proof dish. Sieve icing sugar into basin. Add pinch of salt and egg whites.
Place basin over saucepan of simmering water and whip egg whites until stiff and shiny. Spoon meringue over pears.
Dot with sliced almonds and brown under grill for 5 to 6 minutes. Serve hot.

Apple dumplings from **Upper Normandy**

Ingredients for 4 people:

4 apples,
150 g butter,
300 g flour,
pinch salt and cinnamon,
1 egg,
2 tablespoons redcurrant jelly,
1 liqueur glass Calvados.

Peel and core the apples.

In the centre of each apple put a little butter and a pinch of cinnamon and cook them in a slow oven, in a buttered dish.

In a bowl, rub together the butter, cut into pieces, the flour and a little salt. Then add a little water to obtain a smoother dough.

Form into a ball then flatten with a rolling pin. Fold into quarters and repeat the operation four times. Leave to rest in a cold place for a good quarter of an hour.

To finish, roll out the pastry (to a thickness of 1/2cm) and cut out 4 good circles large enough to wrap the apples in.

Place a cooked apple on each round.

Thin the jelly with a dash of Calvados and fill the centre of each apple with it.

Wrap each apple in its pastry jacket.

In a small bowl, separate the egg yolk from the white and beat the yolk. Brush each dumpling with egg yolk and criss-cross the pastry all over with a fork.

Put the fruit on a baking sheet and cook in a hot oven for 30 minutes.

At the moment of serving, pour the Calvados over and set alight.

Apple dumplings from Upper Normandy

Shortbread biscuits from **Caen**

Ingredients for 6 people:

Shortbread biscuits from Caen

250 g flour,
250 g butter,
125 g caster sugar,
3 eggs,
1 lemon,
pinch salt

Cook the eggs in boiling water for ten minutes. Cool in cold water. Shell them. Separate the yolks from the whites.

Wash and dry the lemon. In a bowl, put the flour, the salt, the sugar and the egg yolks.

Mix well with a fork. Soften the butter and gradually incorporate into the mixture along with the grated rind of the lemon.

Knead well by hand and form into a ball. Cover with a cloth and leave to rest in a cold place for 1 hour.

Roll out the dough with a rolling pin to a thickness of half a centimetre. Cut out large circles with a fluted cutter. Cut them into quarters.

Moisten the baking sheet and place the biscuits on it.

Cook for 7 to 8 minutes in a very hot oven.

Terrinée or **Teurgoule** (Rice pudding)

Ingredients for 4 to 6 people:

2 litres of whole fresh milk,
150 g of carolina rice,
100 g caster sugar,
2 tablespoons cinnamon,
30 g butter,
pinch salt.

Terrinée or Teurgoule

Bring the milk to the boil. Leave to cool down. In a large, ovenproof bowl in glazed earthenware, put the rice, the cinnamon, the sugar and the pinch of salt. Pour over the milk. Stir well.

Put into a hot oven, lower the heat to medium and cook for a good three hours, without stirring. When a decent crust begins to form on the surface, dot it with butter. Serve the pudding very hot.

Yport tart

Ingredients for 6 people:

150 g flour,
80 g butter,
1 egg,
5 g baker's yeast,
1 tablespoon oil,
3 tablespoons milk,
pinch salt

For the filling:
4 sharp apples,
30 g butter,
150 g caster sugar,
80 g flour,
80 g ground almonds,
1 teaspoon cinnamon,
1 tablespoon Calvados,
a bowl of crème fraîche

Mix the yeast with a little warm milk. Tip the flour into a bowl. Make a well in the middle. Into it put the butter, melted, the yeast, the egg, the oil and a pinch of salt.

Rub together quickly, using the tips of the fingers, until a workable mixture is obtained. Leave to rest for an hour in a cool place.

Butter a tart tin and line it with the pastry by hand.

Peel the apples. Remove core and seeds. Cut into thick slices.

In a bowl, mix the flour, the ground almonds, the caster sugar and the cinnamon.

Add the butter cut into small pieces. Flavour with the Calvados.

Arrange the apple slices in the tart tin. Cover with the almond mixture.

Put into a hot oven and bake for 40 minutes.

Serve the tart hot with a bowl of crème fraîche.

Yport tart

Table of Contents

Imprimé en France par Kapp Graphic, Évreux (27)
ISBN 978-2-7373-4152-6 - N° d'éditeur : 5340.04.01.03.12
Dépôt légal : janvier 2007
www.editionsouestfrance.fr